HOWARD PYLE

H.P.

HOWARD PYLE

Introduction by Rowland Elzea

A PEACOCK PRESS/BANTAM BOOK
TORONTO   •   NEW YORK   •   LONDON

An original PEACOCK PRESS/BANTAM BOOK

HOWARD PYLE
Copyright © 1975 by Bantam Books, Inc.
All rights reserved under International and Pan-American Conventions
Library of Congress Catalogue No. 75-5196
Hardcover SBN 0684-14415-8

All of the original works of art by Howard Pyle reproduced in this book
unless otherwise indicated are in the permanent collection of the Delaware
Art Museum, 2301 Kentmere Parkway, Wilmington, Delaware. The collections
of the Museum began in 1912 with the purchase of a large collection of
Pyle's work from his widow. Since that time not only has the collection
been greatly enlarged by purchases and gifts, but other collections
relative to the history of illustration have been formed and are continuing
to grow. The Bancroft English Pre-Raphaelite collection provides material
for the strong English influence on American illustration and the John
Sloan, F. O. C. Darley and Pyle pupil collections are areas of particular
concentration although other areas of illustration are also being collected.
The value of the collections is greatly enhanced by the Museum's library
which has extensive holdings in the field of illustration.

PRINTING HISTORY
First U.S. Edition: August, 1975
Hardcover Edition: August, 1975
Book Design by Robert Blanchard
Hardcover edition published by Charles Scribner's Sons, by
arrangement with Peacock Press, a division of Bantam Books, Inc.

Bantam Books are published by Bantam Books, Inc. Its trademark,
consisting of the words "Bantam Books" and the portrayal of a bantam,
is registered in the United States Patent Office and in other
countries. Marca Registrada.
Bantam Books, Inc., 666 Fifth Avenue, New York, New York 10019

Published simultaneously in the United States and Canada

PRINTED IN THE UNITED STATES OF AMERICA
by Regensteiner Press

INTRODUCTION

oday, with the cinema, photographic illustrations in periodicals and particularly television as our main source of entertainment, it is difficult to imagine the importance of the position reading held as a form of education and diversion in the 19th and early 20th century. The number of people who were literate grew continuously throughout this period, gradually including more and more of the less economically and socially advantaged strata of the population so that by about 1915 the vast majority of people were reading. In response to this growing demand by the literate public, new publishing firms sprang up, cheap mass-circulation periodicals were developed, production and graphic processes were enormously speeded up and delivery methods were radically changed by the formation of a comprehensive postal system.

This tremendous growth made it possible for writers to become commercially successful and for the profession of illustrator to become a well-paying and established one. In a certain sense it could be said that authors and illustrators shared with matinee idols and sports figures the role of folk heroes— discussed, compared, revered and collected. As writers and illustrators became more successful, they had to become more responsive to the changing tastes and demands of their patrons, the reading public. No longer could the gentleman author write at a leisurely pace to please himself, nor could the illustrator indulge his artistic moods at will.

The illustrators were not only accurate portrayers of the self-image and aspirations of the public for whom they worked, but they also went far toward setting the artistic standards for their public at the time. Illustrations were clipped out, framed and hung on the walls to be admired and remembered by all in the family. This dual role of entertainer and enlightener was followed by many fine illustrators at the turn of the century and Howard Pyle was one of the greatest of them.

Pyle was very aware of his responsibility toward his public, adult or child. In a letter, he wrote, "There is a very much higher object achieved in the writing of these children's books in the power that one has of, I will not say shaping, but directing their minds into certain liking of what may be good honest art and good honest literature." In his later years, he also embraced the art of mural painting with a similar idea—that of being able to put forth an uplifting message in a public place to be seen by tens of thousands.

Howard Pyle (1835–1911) was a man of many parts. Not only was he an exceedingly prolific illustrator, having produced over 3,300 published illustrations, or two a week during his working life, but also he was nearly as energetic as a writer with almost two hundred texts to his credit, ranging from short fables for children to his four-part compilation of the King Arthur stories. As if this were not enough, he was a highly influential teacher of illustration. Although the number of his students cannot be determined with certainty, well over 100 studied with him in his classes at the Drexel Institute in Philadelphia from 1894 to 1900 and in his own school in Wilmington, Delaware from 1900 until he went to Italy in late 1910.

The work of his students can be found in the publications of most of the major book and periodical publishers of the first quarter of the 20th century. For example, N. C. Wyeth is known for his "Treasure Island" illustrations and his work for the novels of Kenneth Roberts, Nordhoff and Hall and C. S. Forester,

among many others. Frank Schoonover achieved fame for his portrayals of Hopalong Cassidy as well as of the Indians of the Hudson's Bay area. Clifford Ashley, born in the seaport of New Bedford, Massachusetts, brought first hand knowledge to his whaling subjects, and Gayle Hoskin's western scenes enlivened the covers of western "pulp" adventures, among other stories, for decades. Stanley Arthurs was a specialist in scenes of American history. Jessie Willcox Smith's subjects were round faced and well scrubbed children to warm the hearts of the readers of women's magazines. Leslie Thrasher developed a unique "continued story" in his weekly portrayal of the life of Lil and Sandy on the cover of *Liberty* magazine, which was elaborated by a brief text by Thrasher in every week's issue. All these and many others equally important who devoted their careers to illustration were pupils of Howard Pyle. Somehow, even with all this activity, Pyle managed to fit in a brief period as Art Editor of *McClure's* magazine in 1906 and to paint three major mural decorations for public buildings in Minnesota and New Jersey. One might think that this left him with little time for a family but, on the contrary, he married and was the father of seven children.

Pyle's working career began in 1876 when his first illustration was published in *Scribner's Monthly* magazine. This was reproduced by means of wood engraving as were all of his works until 1887 when some began to be reproduced by photo-mechanical halftone. In 1893 his first work reproduced by the two-color method appeared (the use of one color besides black and white). "In the Wood Carver's Shop" and "Bringing Fire and

Terror to Rooftree and Bed" were done for this technique. Finally, in 1897, his first full color illustration appeared reproduced by the four-color process—that is, the use of separate halftone plates for the red, yellow, blue and black hues of a picture.

Pyle, as a professional illustrator, worked with a knowledge of how his pictures were to be reproduced and adjusted his technique to best utilize the qualities of the particular reproductive method to be used. Much of his early work was done with pen and ink which could be most accurately reproduced by the wood engraver's burin or by line cut as in the Robin Hood and King Arthur subjects reproduced here. Work to be reproduced by shaded or tonal wood engraving or by photographic halftone was usually done in black and white gouache or oil. "Fast Flew the Black-winged Horse" and "Blackbeard's Last Fight" are examples of this method. Not until the color printing process had been developed sufficiently to meet his high standards did Pyle do much work in color. Consequently, nearly all the pictures reproduced in this color plate book were done in the latter half of his life and are, therefore, late works.

The major part of the work done in the first half of his career was for children's books and magazines. Fully a third of his total illustrative output and more than half of his literary work was intended for children. In his work for children can be seen most clearly his tie with the English Arts and Crafts movement. The style of the drawings for these works and his concern with the design and total production of such books as "Robin Hood" show his sympathy with the ideas of Walter Crane and the English Arts and Crafts movement in

general.

"The Flying Dutchman" (front cover) was one of the few published illustrations he did that did not have an accompanying text. It was reproduced as a double page picture in *Collier's Weekly*. The story is told about its painting that it was done during the summer school that Pyle conducted at Chadds Ford, Pennsylvania in 1900 and that the Pyle family handyman, John Weller, posed for the main figure standing on a slanted cellar door with pegs placed on the boards to keep his feet steady. His cape was tied to a willow tree and from time to time the students poured water over the "deck" on which Weller was standing to give the proper reflections.

At times the Pyle family would take their summer vacations on the ocean at Rehoboth Beach, Delaware. There they encountered local legends of buried pirate treasure. The idea that pirates had been there fired Pyle's imagination and many of his pirate pictures were either painted there or painted from sketches made at the beach. "Marooned" exists in three very different versions. The first one was a small black and white oil published in 1887, the second a larger and more romantic version which was not published and the third, also unpublished, is included in this book.

In 1889 Mr. and Mrs. Pyle visited Jamaica. One feels that the effects of brilliant light and luminous tropical shadow which appear in Pyle's illustrations for "The Fate of a Treasure Town" must have been noted by him then and stored up in his mind to be released fifteen years later in the illustrations. Pyle begins his text for this story of the city of Cartagena in the following vivid style:

"A flaming tropical sky of abysmal blue,
    full of the heavy clouds of the torrid zone;

a wonderful sea of sapphire and emerald, creaming to white upon coral beaches; huge mountainous islands, fringed with cocoa-palms and crowned with exotic verdure; stagnant lagoons where the mangroves cover the oozy mud with their dense lush-green foliage, and where a crawling venomous life moves obscurely beneath the snaky roots. Flaming heat; blazing light; teeming life; redundant color—and death lurking ever hidden in the slime of the rivers. Such is nature's background to the life that one time filled the Spanish Main with the drift that floated in broken fragments from the Old World to the New."

"The Ruby of Kishmoor" was another of the pirate tales of which Pyle was also the author. In this, the protagonist is a young Quaker from Philadelphia who is unwittingly embroiled in an affair involving the beautiful daughter of the defunct Captain Keitt, a ruby the size of a pigeon's egg and three murderous pirates. Pyle himself was born a Quaker and a number of his texts have to do with Quaker subjects or have Quaker characters in them. Early in his life however, he had embraced Swedenborgianism and its view of heaven as a continuation of useful work begun on earth. This was an ethic he endeavoured to follow himself and also to propound to his students and in his mystical writings and illustrations.

One of the mystical texts Pyle illustrated was "The Pilgrimage of Truth" by the Danish writer Erik Bogh as translated by Jacob Riis, the newspaper reporter-photographer who did so much to make the public aware of the miserable lives of immigrants in the slums of New York. In the story, the maiden Truth descends from heaven and tries to find a home first with a powerful king whose view is that truth is what he says it is; then with the priests who admit they do not know what truth is but to maintain their power continue to profess to others that they do; then with a politician who uses only that part of truth that will fit his program. Finally Truth enters the house of a fool who protects her from enemies who would like to kill her by saying that she is his wife and that she has a marvelous gift for making her fantasies sound like truth. Her pursuers can accept what she says because they believe her to be a fool and even then they project her observations to other people, never applying the Truth to themselves.

Pyle had been given the text to illustrate by *Harper's*, as Henry Pitz relates in "The Brandywine Tradition," and the solution of how to illustrate "The Pilgrimage of Truth" came to Pyle during the course of a bicycle ride. Pyle, Frank Schoonover and some other students had decided to ride the ten miles from the summer school in Chadds Ford to Wilmington in order to get some lemonade. On the way back Pyle became silent, a sign of deep thought which his students respected. As soon as he returned to his studio, he began to work. His first version of the six illustrations for the story was done on mahogany panels in oil. Unfortunately, the dark mahogany ground made the pictures so dark that they could not be reproduced in a magazine. He then repainted the series in watercolor and in a much more stylized manner than that in which he had first set them down. The watercolors were the version used by *Harper's*, but the version published here is one of the original oils on mahogany.

A very considerable portion of Pyle's fame rests with his illustrations of American Revolutionary war subjects. He had amassed an exhaustive knowledge of the history of the period and the 18th century in general, and he made every effort to insure the historical accuracy of his pictures while bringing life to them by the power of his imagination. In his illustration of "The Battle of Bunker Hill" for Henry Cabot Lodge's "History of the American Revolution," he obtained information from the British Admiralty office as to the details of the uniforms of the particular unit of British marines making the attack, the weather conditions and the number of men who had fallen in the preceding assault, and he painted it in such a way that "you can smell the gunpowder," as he put it. Similarly, he dispatched some of his students to make detailed drawings of the Chew House in the Germantown section of Philadelphia for his "Attack upon the Chew House."

The desire for accuracy of detail extended to his illustrations of medieval subjects also, but manifested itself in a somewhat different manner. Obviously, the amount of accurate historical information available was less for medieval subjects than for colonial and Revolutionary war subjects, although Pyle used such sources as "Meyrick's Ancient Armor" and the "Kulturgeschichtliches Bilderbuch" by Georg Hirth for his visual information, as well as figures taken from the work of Holbein where appropriate. In order to heighten the feeling of historical accuracy, Pyle used a style of drawing in his medieval works for children which resembled the medieval woodcut used in early books. The language he chose for the children's book texts also had a flavor of medieval English. At the turn of the century a vogue for medieval romances written for adults swept the publishing world and Pyle, because of his success with the children's tales, was naturally thought of as an illustrator for them. However, he disliked painting illustrations for these works as they were usually neither historically accurate nor yet totally fanciful, and what was more, were frequently not well written.

While Howard Pyle was one of the greatest illustrators of his time, he shared that pinnacle with such luminaries as Edwin Austin Abbey, A. B. Frost, Charles Dana Gibson, and Frederick Remington. Literally hundreds of other illustrators were only slightly less distinguished. The generation in which Pyle's pupils matured, the first quarter of this century, also included such superb illustrators as Henry Raleigh, May Wilson Preston, John Sloan, Arthur I. Keller, and Maxfield Parrish among, again, hundreds of others of worth.

Much of the work done at this time deserves to be seen again, not only for the visual delight in seeing the imaginative power, the charm, humor and decorative value of the work of these artists, but also because their work is an intimate insight into the ways of life and the minds of a previous generation. Unfortunately, the art of the illustrator has largely disappeared from the pages of our present day books and magazines—with the significant exception of illustrated children's books. One hopes not only to have the chance to see the best turn of the century illustrators in books such as this one, but that our time can again be enlivened by the work of artists drawing for us today.

Rowland Elzea
Curator of Collections
Delaware Art Museum

2) BLACKBEARD'S LAST FIGHT
Jack Ballister's Fortunes, by Howard Pyle
St. Nicholas, July 1895

3) CAPTAIN KEITT
The Ruby of Kishmoor, by Howard Pyle
Harper's Monthly Magazine, Aug. 1907
(from a reproduction)

4) WHICH SHALL BE CAPTAIN?
The Buccaneers, by Don C. Seitz
Harper's Monthly Magazine, Jan. 1911
(from a reproduction)

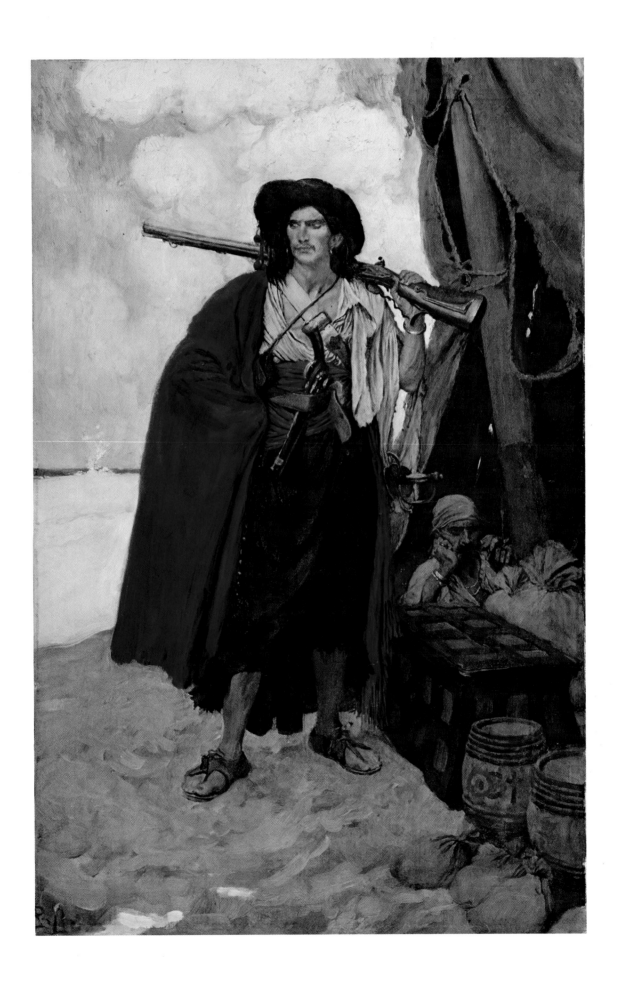

6) AN ATTACK ON A GALLEON
The Fate of a Treasure Town, by Howard Pyle
Harper's Monthly Magazine, Dec. 1905

7) SO THE TREASURE WAS DIVIDED
The Fate of a Treasure Town, by Howard Pyle
Harper's Monthly Magazine, Dec. 1905

8) MAROONED
Not published

11) Study for TRUTH BEFORE THE SEER
The Pilgrimage of Truth, by Erik Bogh
Harper's New Monthly Magazine, Dec. 1900

12) FAST FLEW THE BLACK WINGED HORSE
The Garden Behind the Moon, by Howard Pyle
Charles Scribner's Sons, 1895

13) Study for THE FISHING OF THOR AND HYMIR
North Folk Legends of the Sea, by Howard Pyle
Harper's Monthly Magazine, Jan. 1902

14) THE FAIRY MORGANA
North Folk Legends of the Sea, by Howard Pyle
Harper's Monthly Magazine, Jan. 1902

15) BRINGING FIRE AND TERROR TO ROOFTREE AND BED
The Birds of Cirencester, by Bret Harte
Scribner's Magazine, Jan. 1898

16) ROBIN AND THE TINKER AT THE BLUE BOAR INN
The Merry Adventures of Robin Hood of Great Renown, in Nottinghamshire
by Howard Pyle
Charles Scribner's Sons, 1883
(from a reproduction)

Robin·and·the·Tinker:
at·the·
BLUE·BOAR·INN·

17) THEY QUESTIONED HIM WITH MALEVOLENT PERSISTANCE
The Black Night, by James Hopper
Harper's Monthly Magazine, June 1910

18) THE COMING OF LANCASTER
The Scabbard, by James Branch Cabell
Harper's Monthly Magazine, May 1908

19) NERO HOLDING A GOLDEN LUTE, WITH ROME IN FLAMES
Quo Vadis, by Henryk Sienkiewicz
Little, Brown and Co. 1897

20) PERACTUM EST!
   Quo Vadis, by Henryk Sienkiewicz
   Little, Brown and Co. 1897

21) ON THE EDGE OF THE RING, GUARDED, STOOD
BROTHER BARTHOLOME AND THE CARMELITE
Poisoned Ice, by "Q"
Collier's Weekly, Dec. 17, 1898

22) IN THE WOOD CARVER'S SHOP
By Land and Sea, by Howard Pyle
Harper's New Monthly Magazine, Dec. 1895

23) A WOLF HAD NOT BEEN SEEN AT SALEM FOR THIRTY YEARS
The Salem Wolf, by Howard Pyle
Harper's Monthly Magazine, Dec. 1909

24) THE NATION MAKERS
Collier's Weekly, June 2, 1906
(from a reproduction)

25) THEN THE REAL FIGHT BEGAN
Pennsylvania's Defiance of the United States, by Hampton L. Carson
Harper's Monthly Magazine, Oct. 1908
(from a reproduction)

27) TWO KNIGHTS DO BATTLE BEFORE CAMILARD
The Story of King Arthur and His Knights, by Howard Pyle
St. Nicholas, March, 1903

28) AT THE GATE OF THE CASTLE
Peire Vidal, Troubadour, by Olivia H. Dunbar
Harper's Monthly Magazine, Dec. 1903

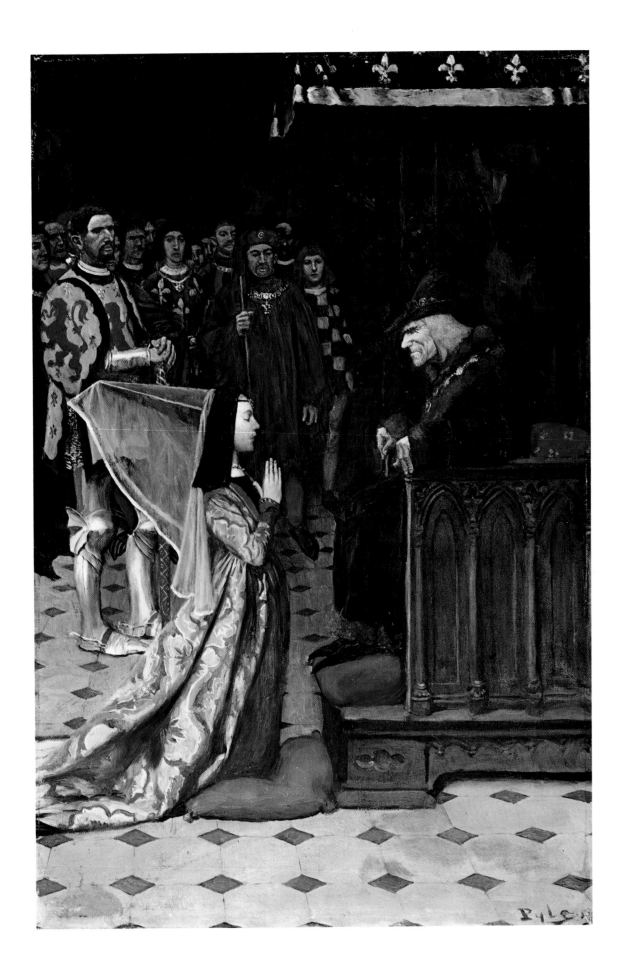

30) HER HEAD AND SHOULDERS HUNG OVER THE SPACE WITHOUT
The Maid of Landevennec, by Justus Miles Forman
Harper's Monthly Magazine, Sept. 1904
(from a reproduction)

32) THE DUEL BETWEEN JOHN BLUMER AND CAZAIO
In the Second April, by James Branch Cabell
Harper's Monthly Magazine, April 1907

34) THE FLYING DUTCHMAN
Collier's Weekly, December 8, 1900

36) THE EVACUATION OF CHARLESTON BY THE BRITISH, DEC. 14, 178
The Story of the Revolution, by Henry Cabot Lodge
Scribner's Magazine, Sept. 1898

37) THE BATTLE OF BUNKER HILL
The Story of the Revolution, by Henry Cabot Lodge
Scribner's Magazine, Feb. 1898

38) WATCHING THE BATTLE FROM THE STEEPLE
Dorothy Q, by Oliver Wendell Holmes
Riverside Press, 1893
(from a reproduction)

40) THE FIGHT ON LEXINGTON COMMON, APRIL 19, 1775
The Story of the Revolution, by Henry Cabot Lodge
Scribner's Magazine, Jan. 1898

41) THOMAS JEFFERSON WRITING THE DECLARATION
OF INDEPENDENCE
The Story of the Revolution, by Henry Cabot Lodge
Scribner's Magazine, March 1898

42) THE ATTACK UPON THE CHEW HOUSE
The Story of the Revolution, by Henry Cabot Lodge
Scribner's Magazine, June 1898

Detail

43) THE ATTACK UPON THE CHEW HOUSE
The Story of the Revolution, by Henry Cabot Lodge
Scribner's Magazine, June 1898